Contents

Introduction

This book accompanies the Bristol Dog School puppy training class, where we only use reward-based methods to teach your dog. We have smaller class numbers that are calmer and are better for learning and easier for us to get to each puppy and give a little more attention.

Reward based training is all about rewarding or paying your dog for a job well done often called Positive reinforcement (+R) this means we add praise and rewards for behaviours we want to encourage and rewards correct behaviour so that unwanted behaviours are not rewarded and are then forgotten this avoids using punishment or aversive training methods.

Rewards are generally food but can be toys or anything that your dog finds rewarding, for some dogs this may be hunting or chasing.

The reason we use reward-based training is because science has proven that an action learned in a nice way that is reinforced with something the dog finds rewarding is leaned and retained for longer, alternatively an action punished may never stop as the punishment may still be rewarding to the dog if all it wants is attention.

During the course you will learn how to get your puppy to sit, stand, lay down, settle, stay, leave items, release items, walk on a loose leash and recall, we also allow pups to try enrichment toys during classes which helps their mental and social development.

The main training technique used is called luring, where the puppy is lured into position and marked using a verbal cue and rewarded. There are other reward based methods that can be used and some are covered in this book, depending on how your dog learns we may chose these other methods in classes.

If you wish to learn more about any of the subjects I have mentioned here please check out the blog on the website:

www.bristoldogschool.co.uk/blog

Laws

The Animal Welfare Act 2006 (amended 2015)

On the 6th April 2016, it became a legal requirement for all dogs to be microchipped. The Animal Welfare Act 2006 (amended 2015) section 12. Is clear that all pups must also be microchipped by the time they are 8 weeks old and all adult dogs should be microchipped as soon as possible. There are no exemptions to this law, unless for specific health reasons, in which case your Veterinary surgeon will have to fill out a form from the secretary of state.

Your Vet will scan your dog when it attends a regular health check, if it is found to not have a microchip then they may report your dog to a local enforcement officer or Dog Warden, although they are not bound to do this.

If your dog is found to not have a microchip then you have 21 days to have microchipped implanted or you will incur a £500 fine, you are also liable for a £500 fine if you do not keep your microchip details up to date on a national database.

Please do not worry the microchip is a little bigger than a grain of rice, it is implanted using a needle and is very quickly done, some dogs react to this some don't feel a thing, but it is a very quick procedure and once done the microchip will not be noticeable.

Control of Dogs Order 1992

There is a legal requirement under the Control of Dogs Order 1992 for you to have a collar or harness tag on your dog when it is out in public, the tag must have your surname, house name and or number, road name and postcode on it. It is also useful to have a contact phone number on the tag, as this will make it easier for you to get your dog back quickly. The only exemption to this law is for working dogs where collars can be a hindrance to them.

The Dangerous Dogs Act 1991.

Section 1 pertains to the ownership of banned or exempted breeds such as the Pitbull.

Section 3 pertains to the control of all dogs while they are in public or in private residences. This section make it an offence for a dog to be out of control. This means dogs should always be on lead while walking on highways (public roads) they should either have a reliable recall or be kept on a lead be it short or long when in open public spaces where they are exercising. They should also be under good control in private residences to ensure they do not hurt a human, and should a person feel threatened by your dog they may also report you to the police.

Local bylaws

Bristol City Council have local bylaws that can see an owner be fined up to £500 if their dog is seen to foul in a public place, park of highway and they do not pick it up.

They also have a list of public open spaces where dogs are not allowed to be off lead including on highways, again an owner may be fined up to £500 if you are in breach of these bylaws.

Useful items for your puppy's training

Place mat – a bathmat can be a good option. We use this to help you encourage your dog to learn to settle, this can then be taken to different location where you can practice.

Kong – Licking and chewing are calming behaviours for dogs the Kong can also be used to provide a meal for your dog. We also use Kong toys to teach certain behaviours in class.

Snuffle mat – sniffing is a calming behaviour the snuffle mat can like the Kong be used in class or at home to provide a meal

Collar – adjustable size as puppies grow quickly – you should be able to easily fit two fingers between it and your dogs neck to ensure if is not too tight. Dog with narrow heads may need a wider Greyhound collar.

Collar tag – This is a legal requirement, tags must have your surname, house name or number, road name and post code on. I also recommend a mobile phone number or two for speed of getting your dog back. I prefer the Indigo collar tags plate tags that slide onto the collar rather than dangly tags that can get caught and fall off and also the engraving wears to unreadable.

Harness – H style harness like the t-touch harness or Y style harness like the perfect fit. The fuffwear harness is also very good particularly If you have an escape artist then the ruffwear Webmaster will be a good choice.

Leash – I like the original halti training leash as it's comfortable in the hands and has two clips should you heed to connect the leash to two points for security with your dog or you would like the leash longer or shorter in different situations. t-touch also sell a similar version of this leash

Long line – these allow your puppy some freedom and safety while they learn recall. They come in various lengths but stick with the 5,10,15 or 20 meter lines.. Remember that the longer the line the less control you will have should your dog decide to bolt because they have the ability to build up speed, Also the longer the leash the more you have to real in and out regularly on a walk.   I like to use biothane lines because they come in bright colours that are easily seen by people and also because they don't soak up water making them easy to clean and quick to dry.

Whistle – I use and sell Acme dog whistles. They have specific pitches for the gundog breeds but you can use them with any breed of dog and they really can make all the difference with your recall.

Training treats

Training treats or rewards should be small so as not to fill up your puppy too quickly, remember a puppy with a full tummy wants to lay down and go to sleep so smaller treats mean you can have more repetitions during training before puppy becomes full or becomes tired.

Training treats can be your dog's normal food, be that kibble or pieces of raw meat or even pieces of fruit or vegetable. Remember food that your dog eats on a regular basis may be less rewarding for it, so for rewarding complicated behaviours like recall or even the most simple of behaviours when there are lots of distractions like other pups or people in a training class we may need to up our treat level. Smelly cheese or hotdog can be ideal for this also liver pate in tubes from local pet stores can be invaluable when teaching your puppy to loose leash walk.

Liver cake is a high value reward that you can make and freeze ready for when you need it, you will also find lots of great recipes on the internet for other healthy training treats that your puppy may enjoy

Treat preference test

What food does your puppy prefer?

Learning about your puppies preferences helps you to reward them when they make the right choice.

www.bristoldogschool.co.uk

Variety is the spice of life!

A varied diet is not only good for your puppy but it can be useful when we are trying to teach our puppy new things particularly if those things are difficult and if we're in a place that's really distracting and of course we all work harder for things that we really like and want.

What's worth £5 and what's worth £1000 to your puppy?

The choice your puppy makes is going to be what reinforces it the most, and this is important if we want our puppy to pay attention to us in really distracting environments, like puppy classes or when out on walks. But how do we know what our puppy likes?

Finding out our puppy's reward preferences

First we need a selection of food rewards below is a list of examples:

Carrot	Apple
Cheese	Bacon
Blueberries	Hot dog
Kibble	Cocktail sausage

Choose two of these foods and take two pieces of those two foods we'll call them food 1 and food 2.

- You will then ask your puppy to sit 3 times
- The first time you will reward with food 1
- The second time you will reward with food 2.
- The third time you will have food 1 in your left hand and food 2 in your right hand and you will bring them down in front of your puppy to sniff so it's knows it has a choice then bring your hands

apart and open them allowing the puppy to choose which food

to take first.

This demonstrates what the puppy's preference is and what it will in turn find the most reinforcing. It also introduces new smells to your puppy and improves the puppy's diet by adding to it.

On the next page you will find a table where you can make a note of the different foods you try and the ones your puppy prefers.

Example

	Food	Preference
1	apple	X
2	carrot	

	Food	Preference
1	carrot	
2	Apple	
1		
2		
1		
2		
1		
2		
1		
2		
1		
2		
1		
2		
1		
2		
1		
2		

Liver cake

1 lb (450g) liver (lamb, pig, chicken)

1 lb (450g) rice flour

3 eggs

2 cloves of garlic (optional)

One teaspoon of oil

Dash of milk

Liquidise liver with eggs, milk, oil and garlic in blender. Add to flour and mix.

Put in an oven proof dish and cook for about 25 mins on 180c

or

Put into a microwave dish and cook on full power for about six-ten minutes.

The cake should bounce back when pressed lightly, when cooked.

Cut the cake into slices and freeze. Take out of freezer when required.

House training

We all want out pups to be going outside for toilets each and every time it needs to go, but of course this is not as easy as it sounds.

Many puppy owners will be using puppy pads or newspaper, which is fine to start with but these need to be phased out quickly or they only teach the puppy that it can toilet inside the house, these can be moved towards the back door so that puppy heads there looking for the mat and this alerts you the owner to their intent allowing you to encourage them outside to toilet, where you can reward them calmly.

Remember the big wide world is big and exciting so once outside puppy may forget what it's out there for and become distracted, allow them time to sniff about they may remember their need or you may end up going back inside where you will need to pay close attention to them to be able to get them back outside when they remember what they initially wanted to go outside for.

As puppies get older their bladder and bowel control gradually increases, this does mean that accidents in the house can happen, these accidents should be quietly cleaned up without fuss. There are some good pet safe cleaning products on the market, or you can dilute biological washing powder with warm water this can then be used to wash the area as it breaks down the enzymes in the urine and removes the smell, so the puppy is less likely to go back to the same location to toilet. You should never rub your puppy's nose in it to teach it a lesson a puppy will not understand this.

There are specific times you should remember to take your puppy outside for toilets, when it wakes up, during and after play and after meals, then you are less likely to get accidents.

Setting an alarm for every hour on the hour to take your puppy outside can also be helpful. Some owners also choose to set an alarm to get up in the night to let their puppy out.

When your puppy goes outside to toilet praise it calmly once it has finished, not during. You can even use a cue word such as "be quick" or "go toilets" that your puppy will start to learn means go to the toilet.

Toilet training can take weeks or months and of course illness can cause setbacks, but please remember to patient with your puppy and be as structured as possible with toilet times.

Basic skills

Sit

The most basic of all things you will teach your puppy, also one of the behaviours we ask of our dogs a lot.

To achieve the sit we place a food reward on the puppy's nose say the word sit and move it back over the puppy's head to that its bottom sits on the ground as its head raises. As soon as the bottom is sitting we mark with the word yes or a click, from a clicker, and deliver the food reward. Some puppys may choose to shuffle backwards to follow the food reward rather than sit, to stop this from happening position the puppy in front of a wall or door so that they cannot move backwards, or you can mark and reward them when they choose to sit themselves, this does involve a lot of watching your puppy to see what behaviours they exhibit during the day and having very good mark and reward timing.

Stand

This is a useful behaviour to teach your puppy, should you need to examine them all over or groom them.

To achieve a stand have the puppy sat or in a down position in front of you, place a food reward on the puppy's nose stay the "stand" cue and gradually move your hand backwards and to your side until the puppy is fully standing up, at this point your mark and reward the behaviour.

Down/settle

Learning to lie down is the start of learning to lie down and settle which is an important thing for your puppy to learn if you want them to be accepted while out and about taking them to the homes of friends and family as well as to your local pub or café.

Some puppies lie down front paws first and others lie down hind paws first. The first time you do this exercise you may well not know which your puppy choses so you can try one method and move to the next depending on which your puppy chooses.

It's a good idea you use a blanket or a mat to give you puppy somewhere to settle this really helps to encourage the behaviour when in other locations.

For a hind down you will need to lure your puppy into a sit first and using the same food reward lure your puppy's nose toward the floor between its front paws you may also need to move the food reward away a toward you a little so that the puppy lays down more comfortably, say the cue "down" and lure the puppy into the down mark and reward the puppy with the food lure.

For puppies that lay down front first you can start from a standing position. Again say "down" place the food lure on the puppy's nose and bring down towards the floor between the puppy's paws and also move it closer to the dogs body you many need to do this in front of a wall to stop the puppy walking backwards, when in position mark and reward.

Similarly to the sit position you can also watch your puppy for behaviours is offers in its own time and mark and reward them as and when they happen, but as already mentioned your observations and timing in marking and rewarding need to be very good for this and often not even the most experienced of trainers has perfected this skill.

Once you have your puppy moving into the down you can start to encourage the settle. The settle position is a C shape where the dog flips to rest on one hip and both hind legs go in the same direction to the side. Now some dogs may struggle with this position due to their shape, for example bulldogs and pugs because they are often quite round and will find it harder. If your puppy can do it, they will find it comfortable and when really relaxed they will roll onto their shoulder and lie out to sleep. This is the position that puppies get the best sleep in because they can properly stretch out.

Start with your puppy in the down position look at the position the hind legs are in, if one leg is sticking out more than the other you will find it easier to lure you puppy's head in that direction. You may also find when doing this that your puppy shows a preference to which side they choose to lie on.

First we're going to make sure your puppy can do this manoeuver.

1. With a piece of food lure your puppy's head around towards its hip and as soon as they flip over give them the food

   Now you know your puppy can do it you can introduce the cue

2. Say the word "**settle**" and lure your puppy with the food and reward them when they move into the settle position.

3. Practice this, it should be easy to practice the cue and movement because puppies rarely stay still for long.

4. Phase out the food in your hand and use your hand to lure your puppy in the down and settle position and then reward afterwards.

5. Now stop using the word "**down**" if you are using it and just say "**settle**" and reward your puppy.

The next step is to get duration – get your puppy to stay there for a while you will need 20 small treats.

6. Lure them into the settle and feed them 10 treats one at a time quickly (as quickly as it takes your puppy to eat each one) before they have the chance to get up.

7. Now we will use the other 10 treats: when you feed the last of the first 10 treats hold off on delivering the first treat of the second 10 treats and make your puppy wait a few seconds before you deliver the treat so that you puppy is having to focus on staying still.

8. Now you can start to work on increasing the duration between rewards which makes your puppy work a little harder to earn their reward.

Teething and play biting

Teething

Puppies generally start teething at around 16 weeks old, but this can vary depending on the size and breed of your dog.   Just like human children puppy teething can be quite uncomfortable for them and they will want to chew to ease the discomfort they're feeling.

We can help them by giving them plenty of things to chew on, carrots are a great natural chew that they can enjoy as a food treat, they can also be frozen to make them harder to chew for larger dogs.

Cotton rag toys or knotted tea towels that have been soaked in water and frozen, ice cubes, frozen kongs are also great because the ice cold helps to numb the gums. Also getting Nylabone chews, rubber chew toys and natural chews such as deer antlers or chew roots will give your puppy something nice and appropriate to chew, rather than seek to relieve its sore gums on your furniture or other belongings.

By the time your puppy is around 6 months old their teeth should be all through and in place.

Older pups also go through a second teething stage as the growth plates in their bones start to fuse - this generally happens around 9-12 months. Teething or chewing can be a sign of pain in a dog of any age and can also be a sign of stress and the puppy wanting to calm itself.

Other biting

Other reasons your puppy may bite other than teething, are playing, frustration, hunger, attention seeking, too hot or too cold excited or tired, or in need of the toilet or in pain. It's best to work out what is causing the behaviour each time so that you know how to remedy the situation for you and your puppy. You may need to feed your puppy or take them out for the toilet or do a little training with them. If your puppy is over excited or over tired giving them calming things to sniff, lick and chew can really help to focus and calm them enough that they settle and go to sleep.

Items you can use are snuffle mats, stuffed kongs, puzzle feeders stuffed hooves or even a dried animal ear or tendon. If your puppy is struggling to calm you may find sitting on the far side of their puppy pen or baby gate will give you the space to sit out of bite range of your puppy but be able to calm them by dripping treats into snuffle matts or feeders. If your puppy is in pain or discomfort, please seek veterinary attention as soon as possible to relieve your puppy.

Loose leash walking

Being able to walk your dog to heal or on a loose leash is probably one of the most desired things for a dog owner. No one wants to be dragged to the park by their dog. Loose leash walking can be a long process for some owners and dogs to learn, but the sooner the learning starts and your puppy is not rewarded by any pulling on lead the easier and faster it can become.

The first thing to do is decide which side you intend to walk your puppy on either the left or right. This is so that you teach the puppy where you want it to be and it doesn't cross in front of you or behind you where it could trip you up.

Get a handful of treats or a tube of liver paste in a tube and encourage your puppy to sit next to you on the side you have decided you want it to learn to walk. Hold the food reward in the hand on the same side as your puppy and have the leash draped in front of you and held in the opposite hand. The leash should always be loose and should look like the letter "J" in shape as it drapes.

Now we know how to hold the leash and position our puppy we can progress to movement. Place the food reward on your puppy's nose and encourage it forward as you step off with the leg nearest your puppy.

Remember body language is important to dogs so moving this leg first is a cue to your puppy that you are about to start walking.

At first you will need to offer a reward for every step you take while your puppy is beside you, this teaches your puppy where you want it to be. If your puppy becomes distracted, you can encourage it back beside you using the food or wait for it to come back once it's ready.

The next step is to build on how many steps can be taken between food rewards. This should be built up slowly a step at a time. Again, start with puppy beside you and encourage them to step off with you and then every other step if they stay with you offer them a food reward. The steps between food rewards can gradually be increased. If you find that at a certain number of steps your puppy starts to become too easily distracted, then decrease the number of steps between food rewards and practice at this level for a longer period of time before increasing the steps gradually again.

You can of course use a **"heal"** or **"close"** cue for your dog this can be useful if you intend to teach your puppy to walk beside you off lead and you want to give it a cue for doing this. If this is not something, you plan to do you can instead just use the lead being attached as the cue for your puppy to understand that it is to walk nicely beside you.

Alone Training

This is one of the most important things you will ever teach your puppy, at some point we will all have to leave our dogs at home, because we need to go shopping or to the doctor's, to a wedding or funeral or we may even need to go into hospital for a time and someone else has to come in and feed and walk our dogs for us.

As responsible dog owners we need to help our dogs learn how to settle and be calm in their own surroundings at home.

The first thing to remember is that we do not allow our puppies to bark or cry in a crate or room - they are very social animals at this age and have probably come from a place where they were with litter mates and their dam being alone is scary at first. What we want to do is let them know that we are there for them and that they can trust us.

You may choose to give your puppy a safe place such as a crate or a puppy pen, this is not only to keep your belongings safe but to keep your puppy safe. Alternatively, you may opt for a specific room that you have puppy proofed with a bed in it, whatever you choose this should be in a quiet place in the house this may be the kitchen or living room. Ensure that the bed or crate is in a draft free place away from direct sunlight, you can get a crate cover or use blankets to make the dog feel more secure. This room or crate must be a place of nice things - feed your puppy in this area, give it treats and toys here and never send your puppy to this place be it a crate or room as a punishment.

Once you have lovely comfortable place for your puppy that you are making positive associations with by using treats or enrichment toys such as stuffed kongs you can start to leave the room your puppy is in and move to another room where you can still hear your puppy. You may also invest in an indoor CCTV camera so that you can watch your puppy. At first your puppy may not like being left at all, so you may not even get out of the door. This is completely understandable your puppy's confidence needs to build slowly over time so you will be working slowly on steps away and creating distance from puppy, this may only be making a cup of tea in the kitchen.

Once you have this calm behaviour in the room or crate start to leave out of the front door this may only be to put some rubbish in your bin but your puppy will see you calmly leave and calmly come back while it is happy playing with a toy or just chilling out in its safe place.

I recommend walking out of the door randomly numerous time during the day so that puppy gets used to leaving and it doesn't become an issue. Once you have a puppy that doesn't react to you walking through the front door you can gradually build up the time outside the front door, this may only be a few seconds at first slowly building to minutes. As you increase your alone time you may choose to take a cup of tea outside with a book to read so that you are close and able to hear or even watch your puppy on your CCTV so that if you notice any kind of distressed behaviour you can go back in side. Seeing distressing behaviour would be a cue to you that you are pushing your puppy too far and you need to take a step back in your along time and not leave the puppy for quite so long.

Again add in new things over time like going for a quick walk around the block or turning the engine of your car on and maybe even leaving your driveway if you have one to going to the shop, so that your puppy gets used to you doing these things and being left alone at home.

If you or your puppy are struggling with this you may need to call on a trainer to help you as some pups just cannot seem to manage when left and often need more structured training and possible help with medication from a vet.

Recall

There are several reasons that recall isn't maintained from the puppy period into the adolescent and adult periods and the dog then learns to ignore the recall cue:

1. The recall cue wasn't conditioned well initially
2. The dog isn't driven enough to respond to the recall cue, this can happen due to the increase in dopamine, that feel good hormone that drives them to keep having an experience they enjoy, such as playing with other dogs or going after a scent.

In short if we don't make our recall training fun enough there isn't going to be a dopamine rush and your puppy is less likely to respond to your recall cue.

We also have to consider that your puppy may not have even heard you. Yes they have far superior hearing compared to us but they have to listen to us humans chatting all day every day and this means that cues at a bit of a distance with other ambient sounds interfering just may not be discerned and heard. We talk a lot it's human nature and how we communicate but when we are outside with our dogs there are other sounds sights and smells (distractions) that our voice has to compete with. Our voice may also not be good enough to cut through some of those other ambient noises, wind, trees rustling, cars, rain, other people talking.

When we add in distance to that it makes it even harder for our Puppy to discern the cues we may be giving them. As such, we may think they are ignoring us when in fact they may genuinely not hear us at all.

Recalling our puppy with a sound that is more unique, that they only hear at certain times, and a sound that carries well cutting through ambient noise is more likely to get the desired effect of a more reliable recall from your puppy.

So how can we do this?

Condition your recall well ...

This means rewarding your puppy with the things that give it that dopamine rush, reward with high value food, toys, play and praise.

Make your recall cue truly sound different...

There really isn't much research into whistles and if they are more effective than verbal cues, but anecdotally they certainly do seem more effective.

What's the best whistle cue to use?

Multiple pips 3+ seem to be the most effective as they are more inviting and fun sounding. Long high-pitched sounds are a bit of an assault to our ears and can also be aversive to the ears of a dog.

The sound is also more unique and clearer as it's only heard in the walking environment, so it's less likely to merge into other sounds

What whistle should you choose?

My preference is the Acme whistle these are all set a specific pitch that cover different distances and are louder or softer.

The Acme 211.5 is for retrievers who range further the Acme 212 also covers distance and is recommended for HPR breeds.

How do we introduce and condition a whistle?

I like to start conditioning by using the whistle when I feed the puppy every meal for at least a week. It doesn't matter that the dog is standing in front of you when you blow and put their food down this exercise is about pairing the sound to a large reward, your puppy's dinner.

Then I like to introduce a recall game that taps into your puppy's natural drive and also makes you more fun thus increasing the dopamine levels.

1. Hold a reward in your hand

2. Pip the whistle (remember the multiple pips)
3. Lure the puppy in and let it sniff the reward while you hold its collar or harness or give it a little fuss.
4. Throw the treat out a few feet, this makes the reward more interesting as we bring in movement and sniffing as the dog searches for the food, these are both parts of a predatory action pattern. Orient – stalk – chase – sniff – consume
5. Repeat each step throwing the treat in different directions and have fun.

Remember don't just call your puppy back at the end of a walk call them back regularly and reward and praise them when they check in (look back) with you.   Call them in play with them, do a little training with them, put their leash on and take it off again etc.

The important thing to remember is not to scold your puppy for making a mistake, as this will have an adverse effect on your recall. If you need a little extra help to keep your puppy safe use a long line so that they can have a bit of controlled freedom.

Swap or drop

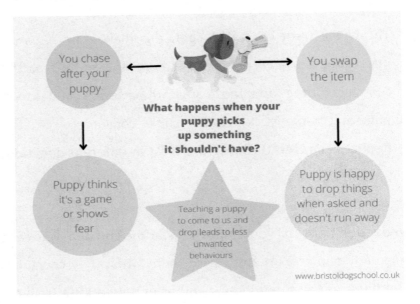

What do you do when your puppy picks up something you don't want it to have or its dangerous for your puppy so you need to remove it from your puppy's mouth quickly?

Puppies like to explore they do this with their eyes, ears, nose and mouth. This means they pick things up that look and/or smell interesting basically to a puppy that is anything that will fit in their mouth.

Our immediate reactions to many things our puppy picks up differ. If it's a puppy toy we don't react, but if it's something they shouldn't have we may react verbally and physically by moving towards them, getting hold of them and then opening their mouth to remove the item (if they're teething this could be rather uncomfortable for them).   What we're teaching them is that the items we don't want them to have are valuable and get our attention and they can instigate a game with us or they may learn to resource guard the item. There is both a genetic link and a learned aspect to this behaviour where you may see your puppy hide and defend items by growling this may then escalate to snapping if growling is ignored or they may consume the item quickly to ensure you cannot get it.

Equally we don't want to totally ignore the behaviour, because some pups will still chew up and consume the items they pick up and this could be dangerous to them.

How do we get items back?

Swapping items and teaching a drop cue is far safer and means that your puppy is less likely run away from you in play or due to fear.

Remember when swapping that the items should be of equal or higher value.   A dry biscuit or piece of kibble is not as valuable to a dog as a meaty bone or dried chew like a pig ear.   We have two ways of teaching a drop - both are valuable for your puppy to learn. The first option is when you puppy is calmer and the second for when your puppy is more excitable and in a playful mood when concentration is harder for them.

Option one – swapping a food toy

Items needed

Stuffed food toy (kong)

Your selection of your puppy's treats (remember to consider the value when choosing the treats you use)

1. Fill the food toy with something nice such as cheese spread, or a bit of meat paste and offer it to your puppy.
2. While your puppy is licking at the food toy show/let them sniff a treat in your hand.
3. In your puppy's line a sight a little distance away drop the treat on the floor. If your puppy leaves the food toy immediately you can jump to step 6. If your puppy does not drop the toy put another piece of food down for it continue to do this up to 5 pieces of food.

4. If your puppy is not encouraged to leave the toy you will need to increase the value of your treats.

5. Practice until your puppy is happy to leave the food toy and reduce the amount of treats you need to encourage them away. This should naturally happen as their understanding grows but you may need to increase the value of the treats.

6. Once your puppy is constantly leaving the food toy for a dropped treat or two introduce the "**drop**" cue by giving them the food toy, saying the word **"drop"** then dropping the food reward

7. Practice – you need your puppy to consistently drop the toy for the treat.

Phase out the lure

8. Say the word **"drop"** then wait for your puppy to drop the toy and look at you before you move them away with a treat and pick up the toy.

Option two - The Swapping game

Items needed

Two toys that you can play tug with – we prefer Tug-E-nuff toys

Some treats

This exercise teaches the drop cue when your puppy may be in a more excited playful state (which is when they're less likely to be able to concentrate) we reward the correct behaviour with the reward of swapping one toy for another and also sometimes for a treat.

1. Hold a toy in each hand show your puppy one toy and hold the other toy behind your back or in a pocket.
2. Encourage your puppy to play with the toy.
3. Once you have a good game of tug happening hold the toy still and reveal the other toy and wiggle it around in your puppy's line of sight so that it draws their attention.
4. Hide the first toy behind your back and play with the second toy.
5. Repeat steps 2-4, before you stop playing with the first toy and bring out the second introduce the cue **"drop"** so that the puppy learns to release the toy and move to another on offer .
6. Practice.
7. Repeat steps 2-5 using your cue **"drop"** then wait for your puppy to drop before you then show them the other toy.

Swapping for food

Items needed

1 toy

Treats (this is an exciting game so remember you may need high value rewards to get your puppy's attention)

1. Encourage your puppy to play with the toy.
2. When you have a good game of tug happing put a treat near your puppy's nose and wait for them to release the toy and take the food.
3. Introduce the **"drop"** cue when your puppy is successfully dropping the toy for the treat.
4. Practice.
5. Phase out the immediate use of the treat by playing with your puppy. Use the **"drop"** cue hold the toy still and wait for your puppy to realise and look at you, then reward your puppy.

Phasing out of the rewards allows you time to get a reward if you are caught off guard with your puppy, but it also means your puppy is learning and working to earn a reward.

You should now have a puppy that understands the drop cue and who doesn't run from you whenever it picks something up.

Exercise and your growing puppy

Getting out and about with your new puppy is an exciting thought for any new owner, and while you may want to go out and share long walks through beautiful landscapes and beaches with your pup, it isn't such a good idea while they are young and still growing.

Taking a puppy for a walk should be about an experience for your puppy rather than getting them from A to B or home to park. There is so much going on outside, sights and smells and sounds, that are always changing. Your puppy will be fascinated by all of this, they need time to take them in and process them if you don't allow them this time they may pull you to do things or stop and sit to take in this information. If your puppy sits it could be that they are tired, they aren't being stubborn. Let them sit, give them time to take things in and then ask them if they would like to carry on. It's important that you don't fall into the trap of bribing them to move because you want them to, all you are teaching them is that they can stop at any time and the treats get better.

Social Media Posts and X-ray images

You may encounter this image popping up on social media it's an x-ray of a 2-week-old puppy. You can see how much the bones need to grow before they meet, and of course a puppy at this age isn't walking yet anyway. You may also have heard that old saying about young animals having more bones that adults, well this is based on the fact that bones have growth plates that only fuse together when they have finished growing. And being careful about exercise levels is important in ensuring these growth plates are not damaged as it could cause deformity.

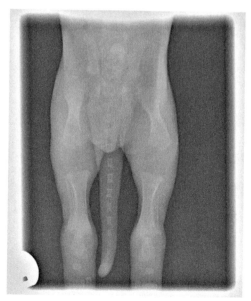

X-ray of a two week old puppy

We must also consider diet, breed and neutering status in the exercise recommendations particularly when some breeds are more predisposed to suffer joint problems such as hip dysplasia and osteochondritis.

Diet must be correctly formulated for your puppy. Large breed puppies should be fed a diet appropriate to slower development. An unbalanced diet too high in nutrients for them can cause growth to speed up to the detriment of your puppy's skeleton. Equally neutering and the removal of the hormones when your puppy is still growing can stunt your puppy's growth or indeed see it to grow too tall, which again will have an effect on joints and tendons.

The 5 minute rule

You may have heard of the **5 minute rule** for walking your puppy.

You walk your puppy for 5 minutes for each month of its age plus 5 minutes twice a day, a three month old puppy would be on 2 x 20 minutes walks per day.

This rule has been designed to reduce the stress of repetitive high impact movement on the growth plates in the hopes that it will reduce the instances of growth plate damage or future joint conditions in older dogs. There have not been any scientific studies to substantiate these claims. Krontveit *et al* (2012) However studied the effects of off lead exercise on pups up to 3 months old and the instances of hip dysplasia (HD). They found that exercise on softer undulating ground decreased the instances of HD development, but if puppies were allowed access to stairs this increased the instances of HD.

When can I do some sports with my puppy?

When your puppy is around 12-18 month of age the exercise you offer can be unrestricted. High impact games such as playing fetch with a ball or agility or flyball should not be considered until dogs are more physically mature. Chasing after a ball can become an obsessive behaviour and certainly in young dogs the twisting, turning and jumping of these high impact sports can put extra pressure on joints that are still forming. Sniffing, searching and retrieve games can be better for a younger puppy to play they get exercise and enrichment for mental stimulation. However you can often work on the foundations of these sports in a more controlled manner and many sports trainers run classes for puppies to help them learn those foundations.

In summary

The 5 minute rule although not studied for its effects may well reduce the instances of joint problems if it is grouped with good diet and neutering at the appropriate time after growth has ended. You may need to do some research on the growth rate of your puppy and your vet or breeder may be able to help you with this. Larger dogs grow slowly and may not finish growth plate fusion until around 18 months - 2 years, whereas, smaller dogs may have finished this before they are 12 months. This is why dog sports have recommended ages that dogs should reach before they can start the more high impact aspects of the sport. This 5 minute rule could also be added to allow your puppy's off lead time to be longer. Free play on softer land such as parks or fields where your puppy will spend time not only exercising muscles and teaching itself about co-ordination, but also socialising, habituating and learning about their surroundings.

As mentioned earlier the start a walk is an experience and all about running around and playing as well as stopping and sniffing and picking up on all those pee-mails and smelling the roses.

When should I get my dog Neutered?

In classes I am always asked about neutering puppies, when is the right time and what might happen to my puppy?

My answer is always to do some research, watch your pyppy's behaviour and consider things such a diet and training and socialisation. Neutering is certainly not the cure all to behaviour and illness that people previously thought.

What Vets Say...

The main thing is yes castration and spaying procedures do stop procreation, but so can keeping in season bitches under close control and away from lothario males.

Some vets tell you that neutering your dog will stop behaviour problems and stop illness,
Some will say get a bitch spayed before she has a season and others will say get a bitch spayed after her first season. Most vets will tell you a

bitch is less likely to get cancer and that she won't get pyometra (a serious womb infection) if spayed.

However, research tells us that there is no significant difference in occurrences of other diseases between neutered and unneutered bitches.

Some vets tell you that neutering your dog will stop behaviour problems, and stop illness, and occurrences of other diseases between neutered and unneutered bitches.

The advice is similar for dogs, some vets say get them neutered before they start to cock their leg, others say get them neutered once they're a year old, as it will reduce the chances of testicular cancer or prostate problems (which happen in later life). Again, research tells us that there is no significant difference in occurrences of other diseases between neutered and unneutered dogs.

Some vets will say it's entirely up to you and are happy to chat to you about the pros and cons and will be warts and all with you, (now that's my kind of vet). Some vets may be behaviourally aware also, if you have this type of vet you are very lucky.

What is neutering?

Neutering is the removal of the sex organs, the testes and ovaries. Often called spaying for bitches and castration for dogs. These sex organs release hormones that travel around the body, primarily Testosterone in males and Oestrogen in females. Hormones travel around the body to the brain where they are regulated by the hypothalamic pituitary adrenal axis or the (HPA axis) the hypothalamus and pituitary glands are in the brain the adrenal gland is on the kidneys. These glands control a lot of what is going on the body, such as stress reactions as well as other body functions, such as growth, it maintains the bodies muscle mass and also energy levels.

The early removal of the sex organs can have a detrimental affect on your puppy, the removal of the hormones mean the body doesn't know when to stop growing, so overgrowth of the joints can happen. It can also lead to dogs that put on weight easily.

So why is overgrowth a problem?

If the bones grow too long it can weaken them and put extra pressure on the joints, this can then lead to early onset arthritis or ligament ruptures.

What affect does the HPA axis have on behaviour?

As already mentioned the HPA axis controls stress reactions. Without the hormones needed these stress reactions can be heightened leading to a dog that is stressed a lot and this can lead to reactive aggression either as a fear response or stress response.

What affect does neutering have on training your dog?

Research has shown that neutered dogs can be more difficult to train.

What if you leave neutering your dog until it is mature?

This is recommended, letting your dog mature naturally will allow the body and hormones to do what they need to and reduce the chances of any growth defects or reactive behaviours surfacing.

If and when you do get your dog neutered you may start to notice changes in it, these don't happen overnight hormones dissipate over the course of weeks. You may notice your dog puts on weight, becomes less energetic (owners - quite often like this) but you do have to increase exercise somehow or reduce the food intake. Females may also become incontinent, because the removal of the hormones causes the bladder sphincter to weaken.

Your dog may also become less confident or reactive towards things that before it was perfectly fine with.

What if you do notice problems?

Some problems can be controlled with hormone replacement medications, so you if you notice any changes in your dog after neutering then it is important that you speak to your vet about potential hormone therapies, and if you see any behavioural changes then you should consult a behaviourist who can work alongside your vet.

Socialisation: What it means and what effect it can have on your puppy?

The dictionary describes socialisation in two ways:

1. The activity of mixing socially with others. *"socialisation with students has helped her communication skills"*

2. The process of learning to behave in a way that is acceptable to society. *"pre-school starts the process of socialisation"*

In short socialisation is about experiencing things and spending time with others to make you more able to cope and exist in society.

When does socialisation start?
Puppies are born deaf and blind, the first 3 weeks of life for a puppy are about filial imprinting with their mother and siblings.

As they grow they enter new stages known as critical learning/sensitive periods.

The first socialisation period is from 4-14 weeks when puppies are weaning. Puppy's senses are developing, they'll be venturing out of the whelping box playing, exploring, maybe going to the vet for the first time. Them at around 8 weeks old they'll be leaving their litter mates, going to new homes and possibly starting to attend puppy training classes.

The second period is the Juvenile/enrichment socialisation period this lasts from 14 weeks to 6 months (sometimes longer depending on the type of dog). This stage is sometimes called the teenage or adolescent stage as your puppy will undergo hormone and physical growth surges. They'll still be learning, their world will still be increasing in size every day, they will be experiencing new things and may still be attending puppy classes or adolescent classes.

During their critical periods puppies are sponges for information and this is the time we should be helping them to learn what is and isn't acceptable. However, socialisation doesn't stop after the critical periods end it carries on through life, but giving them good socialisation experiences when young means they are better able to cope with new things as older dogs.

What is socialisation meant to be and what problems may we see?

The socialisation and juvenile periods are where I start to see confusion in what suitable socialisation is for puppies. So many new puppy owners think that socialisation only means letting their puppy play with other dogs, I so often hear "I don't want "My puppy to be scared or aggressive so I let him play with all the dogs in the park, but he just won't come back when he's called" or "I let him play with all the dogs in the park and he used to come back to me when I called him, but now he ignores me and just won't come back" or my puppy is just so scared of other dogs he hides behind my legs or runs away and I don't know why we go to puppy parties they're not helping".

These owners often think that socialisation with other dogs is letting their little puppy play with all dogs they meet, of course puppies do need to meet and play with other dogs of all ages so that they can learn and grow, but this socialisation needs to be carefully considered.

What most people think socialisation is

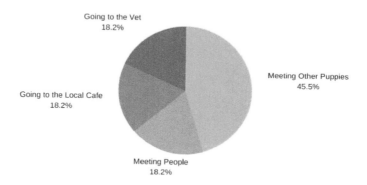

Going to the Vet
18.2%

Going to the Local Cafe
18.2%

Meeting Other Puppies
45.5%

Meeting People
18.2%

What is socialisation meant to be?

Socialisation is really about letting your puppy experience as much social contact with humans of different types, other dogs and other pets as possible, but in smaller doses with a positive outcome. Remember it's about **quality** not quantity. Socialisation also encompasses habituation to new experiences, for example, hearing the vacuum cleaner for 10 seconds is adequate at first and your puppy should be calmly praised and fussed and rewarded so that the vacuum is not a scary noisy thing but the precursor to something nice for the puppy. This could then be repeated a few days later in the same manner.   You may find that the first time your puppy experiences the sound and seeing the vacuum it's particularly interested, but the second it's less interested.

What Socialisation actually is... or should be....

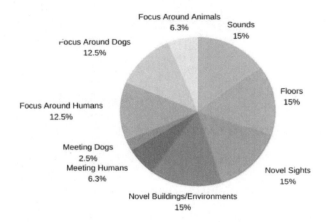

What about puppy classes or parties?

Puppy training classes aren't generally called puppy parties, parties are put on to let puppies play in social groups and often there is little control and puppies can become stressed.

A good training class will not encourage pups to play in groups, it will be run by an experienced and qualified trainer who may have some organisational affiliation or not. They should use reward based methods and will encourage you to bond and learn and play with your puppy while other puppies and people are around. Letting puppies play in groups with no proper control can lead to some puppies becoming nervous of other dogs and others becoming overly confident and almost bullying the less confident puppies. If there is social contact in a puppy class then generally the trainer will only match pups in no more than pairs for a short, controlled period.

Socialisation on walks

Allowing your puppy to run up to and play with every dog on walks teaches it that it is allowed to run up to every dog and encourage it to play. However not every dog wants to play or is able to play. In particular, think of dogs on leads, some may be elderly or frail, ill or recovering from injury and possible surgery and some may be just too scared of others to be able to cope with social greetings and react out of fear. As a result of some of these interactions your puppy may learn to run up to other dogs and defend itself before a proper social meeting has taken place with the other dog.

How do we remedy this?

Interacting with your puppy on walks is paramount. I so often hear "I got a puppy to get me out and about and enjoy walks with", but when these people are on walks the puppy is off elsewhere making their own fun or the owner is on their phone paying little attention to what their puppy is doing.

Playing little find it games with toys, laying scent trails with treats or playing controlled retrieve games and even doing some training are all great ways to interact with your puppy on walks.

And then there is the rule of 3

1. You must stay with me

2. You can say hello

3. You can play with

This is a great rule to follow it allows your puppy to socialise in different ways but also teaches it that sometimes it's not appropriate to say hello, and this is where you will find your puppy's recall improves.

Making a socialisation plan

Vaccinations and not being able to take puppy out until a week after they have finished is often sighted as the reason a puppies socialisation is suspended, but this needn't mean you can't take your puppy out and socialise it or start a puppy training class. You can now get puppy carrying bags, so that they go out with you before they are able to head out on walks on a lead. Your puppy can be carried by you while you sit outside of supermarkets and let them see people and cars or you could just sit outside your house. I used a normal rucksack to carry my puppy and he joined me on my walks with my older dog, so he got to experience everything we did.

Clair carrying Atum in a ruck sack on a walk

I also make a plan, what are all the things that puppy may encounter as it grows up, and you can tick them off each time they encounter them.

On the next page a plan has been started for you with some ideas to get you started along with some empty spaces for you to add things that you may think of that are important for you to have your puppy experience and be happy with.

Anything can be listed so they can be ticked off each time your puppy encounters them. You can keep adding new things all the time and you know that you may have to encounter them again just to make sure your puppy is getting used to them.

Puppy trainers

Enlisting the help of a force free puppy trainer even before you bring your puppy home, will help you start off on the right foot. They can go through important socialisation with you and help you write your socialisation plan, some may also be able to discuss harnesses and diet with you.

Socialisation plan

Experience	1	2	3	4
Motor vehicles	✓	✓	✓	✓
Runners	✓	✓	✓	✓
Cyclists	✓	✓	✓	✓
People in hats	✓	✓	✓	✓
People in sunglasses				
Road works	✓			
Cafes	✓	✓	✓	
Pubs				
Childrens play parks				
Hairdryers				
Vacuum cleaners	✓	✓	✓	✓
Horses	✓	✓	✓	
Cows				
Sheep				
Motor bike helmet on Tim	✓			

Examining your puppy

This is about making handling in any situation a nice experience for your puppy. It may need to be handled by another person, vet, vet nurse, groomer, dog walker or pet sitter and if your puppy is used to this it is more pleasurable for them and hopefully a stress free experience.

Your puppy being used to full body check overs make it easier to do simple daily health checky, you may notice a lump or sticky buds or even a tick on your puppy when you are running your hands over it. Doing this will also allow you to feel for any matts in fur if your puppy has longer fur or it means you are able to avoid matting by employing a daily grooming routine.

This is also the time you can look inside ears to make sure they are clean - a little wax is okay but lots could mean there is an infection or allergy. Eyes should also be clear and bright with no discharge, of course some dogs do have tear staining, this is acceptable.

Teeth should be clean, older dogs do often have some discolouration, but plaque buildup is not good and would need to be removed by a vet. You can start to clean your pups teeth, which means you are less likely to have a dental issue. While cleaning teeth you can also ensure the teeth are not broken, and gums have no sores or bleeding.

Feet and claws: pads should be dry but not cracked and red or sore, and claws should be short and not split. Many dogs do wear their claws down while walking, but some do not and need to have their claws cut regularly to ensure they can walk properly and without discomfort.

Anything you notice that is not normal for your dog should be reported to your vet.

Licky matts or stuffed enrichment toys that can be stuck to a door are great for keeping your puppy's attention while you check them over and this also means they are being reinforced for allowing you to do this, likewise when a vet or groomer handles your puppy give it plenty of rewards so that it sees the attention as rewarding and positive.

Some dogs are more fearful and may react badly to being touched. If this is the case a period of desensitization and behaviour modification training with a trainer or behaviourist, who can advise more specifically on voluntary behaviour modification is required.

Using your puppy's brain

There are plenty of things to you do you use your puppy's brain, training and teaching it basic commands are just one aspect of this.

You can teach your puppy to play games like find it, have a toy that your puppy loves and you only use for that special find it game, hide it somewhere in our house or garden and send you dog off to find it using it's nose, or play the Cup game, using some plant pots. Hide a treat under one and get your dog to use its nose to find the treat. A simple cardboard box with newspaper can be great way to engage you puppy's brain or a snuffle mat that you can hide treats in.

Nina Ottoson has some great puzzle toys, which increase in complexity as dogs get better at figuring them out.

You can also teach your puppy tricks like spin or paw. The American dog trainer Kyra Sundance has written a lovely book called 101 dog tricks, which is full of fabulous ideas you can try.

Alternatively you may want to try specific training like Agility, Hoopers, Rally Canicross or if you have a gundog some gundog training. Please remember you may find that you have to wait for your puppy to have stopped growing to undertake some activities. Teaching your puppy to swim, giving them a sand pit to dig in or find treats in, a paddling pool to splash about in or even giving them a ball pit to play in are some fabulous options too.

Facebook groups can also be a good place to find new enrichment ideas to try out with your puppy.

Getting to know your puppy's body language

Getting to know your Puppy's body language and what it means will really help you to understand when they are happy, anxious or in pain, when social situations are okay or not okay for them and allow you to make appropriate changes for them. Some breeds are slightly different to others due to their physical differences, for instance breeds with no tail like the Boston Terrier, may wiggle their back end still but that wiggle could be out of excitement or anxiety. The flat faced breeds like bulldogs and pugs who may look like they have permanent whale eye because they have large prominent eyes. We often have to look at multiple things our dog is doing to decipher their emotional state at that time. Many of the beautifully drawn behaviours seen on the next page may be grouped together for your dog. They may have their own little way of doing things that you will grow to understand as you spend more time with your dog seeing how it reacts in each situation your knowledge of his emotional state will grow.

On the next page you will see pictorial Descriptions illustrated by Lili Chin of dog behaviour and what each one means.

DOGGIE LANGUAGE

starring Boogie the Boston Terrier

ALERT

SUSPICIOUS

ANXIOUS

THREATENED

ANGRY

"PEACE!"
look away/head turn

STRESSED
yawn

STRESSED
nose lick

"PEACE!"
sniff ground

"RESPECT!"
turn & walk away

"NEED SPACE"
whale eye

STALKING

STRESSED
scratching

STRESS RELEASE
shake off

RELAXED
soft ears, blinky eyes

"RESPECT!"
offer his back

FRIENDLY & POLITE
curved body

FRIENDLY

"PRETTY PLEASE"
round puppy face

"I'M YOUR LOVEBUG"
belly-rub pose

"HELLO I LOVE YOU!"
greeting stretch

"I'M FRIENDLY!"
play bow

"READY!"
prey bow

"YOU WILL FEED ME"

CURIOUS
head tilt

HAPPY
(or hot)

OVERJOYED
wiggly

"MMMM...."

"I LOVE YOU,
DON'T STOP"

7

A word of warning (things to avoid)

Christmas cake/pudding/pies

All contain raisins, currants and sultanas which are toxic to dogs and lead to kidney failure and possible death and alcohol which is also causes sickness

Stuffing

Stuffing containing onion breaks down blood cells and causes anemia stopping oxygen traveling around the body leading to eventual death if not treated

Christmas food to keep away from your dog

Cooked bones

These have little nutritional value and will splinter when chewed which could lead to a perforated stomach and intestines

Macadamia nuts

Cause severe vomiting and muscle weakness

Chocolate

Contains Theobromine which effects a dogs central nervous system, heart and lungs, They will become sick and struggle to breathe and have an increased heart rate this can lead to death

www.bristoldogschool.co.uk

There are things that you should endeavor to keep away from your puppy most of them are foods, some are not, but your dog will attempt to chew and or consume them, which could lead to poisoning or internal blockage/ injury.

Item	Symptoms	Severity
Xylitol – sweetener used instead of sugar often used in chewing gum	Seizures and liver failure	Can cause death
Alcohol	Low sugar levels. low body temperature and low blood pressure	Severe illness
Rasins, currants, sultanas, Grapes - fruit cakes, and Puddings particularly seen at Christmas	Kidney failure	Severe illness possible death
Chocolate /Theobromine	Affects the central nervous system, heart and respiratory system	Leads to death
Macadamia nuts	Causes severe vomiting and muscle weakness	Illness
Caffeine	Affects the heart and causes seizures	Illness

Cooked bones	No nutritional value, splintering can cause perforated stomach and/or intestines. They may also impact inside the intestines causing a blockage	Severe illness and possible death
Cinnamon	Not poisonous but causes difficulty in breathing	Mild
Avocado	Severe vomiting and muscle weakness	Mild
Onion (Alium)	Breaks down blood cells causing anemia reducing oxygen in the body	Severe illness possible death
Antifreeze	Very sweet and should your dog lick any it can cause kidney failure and death.	Severe illness and death
Sticks	Most sticks splinter when chewed possibly leaving splinters in the mouth. If	Can lead the death

	these are consumed they can perforate the stomach and intestines	

Caveats

Item	Symptom	Severity
Garlic	A great natural anti-bacterial and is often used as and anti-parasitic to keep fleas away.	Is toxic to dogs when in very high doses (Lee *et al,* 2000).
Raw bones	They don't splinter in the same way as cooked bones do, and have a lot of nutritional content.	Too much bone in the diet can still cause compaction and chewing on large leg bones can cause dental fractures.

Bristol dog walks

Velvet bottom

Formerly a Roman lead mine, this was abandoned in the Victorian age and since then has been turned into a nature reserve, there is a lovely stone path running through it but there are sometimes sheep grazing.
http://www.somersetwildlife.org/cheddar
Satnav postcode is BS40 7XR

Greyfields Wood, High Littleton

There is a large turning on the left, turn down it and go along a rather bumpy gravel track there is room for around 4 or 5 cars to park. This is a lovely cool woodland walk and the woodland is full of Bluebells in May/June, there is also a very picturesque waterfall leading into a lovely stream perfect for keeping your dog hydrated and cool in warmer weather.
Satnav postcode is BS39 6YE

Felton Common

Parking is by St Katherine's church. Please be respectful of the church and park on the right opposite the church and not on the concrete drive in front of it on during services.

Satnav postcode is BS40 9US

Berrow Beach

Parking is on the beach all year round, it's free in the winter but there is a charge in the summer please check for up to date charges.

http://www.burnham-on-sea.com/beach-safety-tips.shtml

Satnav postcode is TA8 2QX

Brean Beach

Parking in on the beach or in a car park there is a charge for the day please check for up to date charge.

Satnav postcode is TA8 2RS

Sandy Bay

This beach is 2 miles North of Weston Super Mare, it's dog friendly all year round with a free car park.

Satnav postcode is BS22 9UR

Ashton Court

A manor house first built in the 1400's it's set in an 850 acre estate, which also has two deer parks, a golf course and a working model railway. It has a number of ponds ideal for water loving dogs, the manor house is used for functions, but it has a lovely café with indoor and outdoor seating areas and a public toilet.

Please be aware that the estate is used for various events over the course of the year, which means that car parks may be full or closed and also may restrict your use of the whole estate, please check the estate website for information on these events.

www.bristol.gov.uk/web/ashton-court-mansion

There are 3 car parks situated on Kennel Lodge Road, Rownham Hill and Clarken Coombe, there is a charge for parking.

Satnav postcode is BS41 9JN

Blaise Castle

An 18th century manor house set in 650 acres of forest and parkland, it has a stream running through it with waterfalls and ponds and a grade 2 listed castle in the grounds. www.bristolmuseums.org.uk/blaise-castle-house-museum/

There is a charge for parking.

Satnav postcode is BS10 7QT

Troopers Hill Nature Reserve

Troopers Hill is situated in St George, East Bristol, between the A431 Air

Balloon Road and Crews Hole Road. These roads are linked by Troopers Hill Road, from which there are four pedestrian entrances on to the site. You can also cross Troopers Hill field from Summerhill Terrace and Malvern Road (best for wheelchair access) to reach the hill.

Satnav postcode is BS5 8XX

Leigh Woods

Broad leaf woodland running alongside Avon Gorge, with pathway running through it.

www.nationaltrust.org.uk/leigh-woods

There is a charge for parking.

Satnav postcode is BS8 3QB

Tyntesfield estate

Dogs are not allowed into the formal grounds or buildings please check their website. However, there are dog walks around the grounds specified by Tyntesfield.

There is a parking charge.

http://www.nationaltrust.org.uk/tyntesfield/dog-owners/

Wraxall, Bristol, BS48 1NX

Snuff Mills

A lovely woodland walk along a stream with a number of places deep enough for dogs to swim, Please be, aware that only the strongest of dog swimmers should enter the water in certain places as there are a number of waterfalls and weirs that are very fast flowing. There is a lovely café with outdoor seating and a public toilet in the car park.

There is a parking charge.

Satnav postcode is BS16 2HH

Printed in Great Britain
by Amazon

85068901R00045